Annapurna

Gastronomic delights from my Fiji Indian childhood

by

Nalini Naidu

© Copyright 2019 Nalini Naidu

Nalini Naidu asserts her moral right to be identified as the author of this work.

All rights reserved. No part of this publication may be produced or transmitted in any form or by any means, electronic or mechanical, including photocopying, recording or information storage and retrieval systems, without permission in writing from the copyright holder.

Published by Anni Publishing
First published by Zeus Publications 2018

Contact: https://www.facebook.com/fijiindiancookbook/

A catalogue record for this book is available from the National Library of Australia.

Dedication

To Mum, Dad, Anouschka and Nitasha, with love

Annapurna is the goddess

who blesses us with food

and is the source of all nourishment.

Table of Contents

PREFACE..1

A CELEBRATION...3

HISTORY OF CURRY..7

WHAT *IS* CURRY?..11

IN INDIA..15

INDIANS IN FIJI..17

MY HOME...19

FIJI INDIAN CUISINE..23

ECLECTIC INSPIRATIONS..27

FESTIVALS..33

RECIPES..35

    SNACKS/ENTRÉE..37

        Dhokla..38

        Bhajia or Pakora..39

        Seafood Pakora..40

        Samosa..41

        Saina...43

        Upmao...45

        Corn fritters..46

        Kakoda..47

    MEAT/FISH/EGG...51

        Egg Curry..52

        Pulau..53

        Chicken Curry...54

        Lamb Curry...55

- Fish Curry 56
- Fried Fish 57

VEGETABLES 59
- Potato Curry 60
- Pumpkin Curry 61
- Chickpea Curry 62
- Tomato and Bean Chutney 63
- Dhal 64
- Kadhi 65
- Sambhaar 66
- Rasam 67
- Palusami 68

ACCOMPANIMENTS 71
- Avocado Chutney/Dip 72
- Coriander or Mint Chutney 72
- Tomato and Cucumber Salad 73
- Raita 73
- Chilli Relish 74
- Carrot Pickle 75
- Coconut Chutney 76
- Tamarind Chutney 77

RICE/BREADS 79
- Plain Rice 80
- Khicheri 82
- Roti or Chapati 83
- Puri 84
- Savoury Puri 85
- Bhatura 86
- Idli 87
- Dosa 88

- DESSERT/SWEETS 91
  - Easy Fruit Cake 92
  - One Egg Sponge Cake 93
  - Banana Cake 94
  - Scones 95
  - Corny Biscuits 96
  - American Crunch 97
  - Gulgula 98
  - Gulab Jamun 99
  - Barfi 100
  - Suji Ladoo 101
  - Sewai 102
  - Kheer 103
  - Halwa 104
  - Semolina Pudding 105
  - Lakri Mithai 106
  - Kulfi 107
  - Payasam 108
  - Semolina Payasam 109
  - Vakalolo 110
  - Purini 111
- MASALA 113
  - Curry Powder 114
  - Garam Masala 114
  - Tea Masala 115
- BEVERAGES 117
  - Masala Chai 118
  - Pineapple and Mint Juice 118
  - Nimbu Pani or Sharbat 119
- REMEDIES 121

    Cough Mixture 122
    Cough Syrup 122
MENU PLANNER 125
THE MASTER CHEF 129
GLOSSARY: HERBS AND SPICES 133
REFERENCES 139
ABOUT THE AUTHOR 141
ACKNOWLEDGEMENTS 143

PREFACE

The words 'India' or 'Indian' are used to refer to what is present-day India, Pakistan and Bangladesh. Prior to British rule, such countries did not exist and India was comprised of states and provinces. For simplification, I have used India to include the other two countries which are included in the subcontinent. With respect to the 'Indian' community in Fiji, I have referred to them as Fiji Indians.

Cooking in India dates back centuries and constitutes the intermingling of various nationalities. The result is a product which is often a complex influence of cultures, religion, climate and preferences. It is essential to trace the history of food and influences in India to appreciate how present-day Indian food in Fiji is presented. Fortunately, food culture is transportable. We can see that in Fiji, regional Indian food has crossed boundaries in some instances and in others remained closer to their origin. Nevertheless, a cuisine has evolved in Fiji that is quite typical of the diaspora, which includes adopting of ingredients from the local surroundings.

The contribution of the Fiji Indians to Fiji's growth and development is endless, not to forget the unique cuisine that was introduced as they assimilated in their adopted country – a cuisine thoroughly appreciated by all communities in Fiji.

A CELEBRATION

Food is a universal experience. For my readers, I hope this book is a cultural journey that will be rewarded with recipes, cooking tips and the history of Indian cuisine in Fiji.

In applauding the cooking and sharing of food, I invite you on an adventure to gain inspiration to experiment and create. The recipes I have in this collection comprise some family favourites rather than a comprehensive collection of recipes on Indian cuisine.

At a time when it seems we have given up cooking, why write another cookbook? For me, it is simply a celebration of my heritage. Spices permeated my childhood home; the sensual art of cooking with different fragrances, textures and colours combined to create intricate dishes. Aromas of a hearty lamb or goat curry bubbling with curry leaves wafted through the rooms. Dishes would be loaded with a concoction of spices such as fenugreek, cumin and mustard seeds for vegetarian foods. Savouring the delights of the meal, we would mop the flavour-filled sauces with remains of roti, as chapatti is referred to in Fiji.

It is useful to know what cooks are attempting to do with basic flavours as well as textures in their creations. Understanding these basics is an essential requirement to being able to cook. I am of the belief that one can appreciate or write about food as long as there is a deep interest and not necessarily a long tradition of the art with the female members of the family. Food preparation on the whole was not always a female domain, as Dad would visit the market and prepare fish or meat for cooking, not forgetting his role as the best 'taster'.

The copious feasts Mum presented in a ceremonious occasion, whilst observing others enjoying them, gave her profound satisfaction. For the guest, the feast was symbolic of love and devotion – food prepared meticulously and with beguiling enthusiasm for someone special.

Apart from pure nourishment, cooking is many things – creation exercise, use of science, mental diversion, display of love and support and on a bigger scale, an agent for social change. When a friend is sick, it is a nice gesture to care for the friend as well as the family by providing home-cooked meals. Such expressions of kindness hopefully benefits friends in grief and fear. On one occasion, when I learnt that my neighbour's son was very ill, I promptly baked a lemon cake, a family favourite, for my children to deliver. After delivering the gift, they returned home sullen, announcing that they had been placed in an awkward situation. In this instance, the young man had broken his jaw in an accident and was being fed with a straw. I assured them that the cake would be appreciated by other members of the family.

Our home was open to one and all; thus, entertaining family and friends was a frequent occurrence. My parents took a great deal of pride in planning menus to accommodate all and the whole family was often engaged in preparation and service. The spacious balcony was well suited to the many cocktail parties we gave. It was also a tranquil spot for Dad to unwind with his family and often friends at the end of a work day. Watching the boats entering Lautoka Harbour and gazing at the mountains surrounding our home was mesmerising for Dad.

HISTORY OF CURRY

When the Mughal, Babur (1483-1530) came to Hindustan as Northern India was then known, he found the food tasteless and uninteresting. He came from a culture which took a lot of delight in eating. He was used to hearty, meaty dishes such as kebabs roasted over a campfire, having spent a large part of his life in the mountains. This desire conflicted with the dietary habits of the Hindustanis who took a dignified approach to food. Hindustanis were in contempt of food as an earthly pleasure, as for them food was a vital part of the relationship with the gods. 'Annapurna' is an offering for any occasion – religious, social or the need for nourishment. The restrictions and methodology relating to food consumption including meat, particularly beef being prohibited for higher castes, continue absolutely to the present times. Many high-caste Hindus do not eat spicy food as they believe this interferes with rational thought.

'Ayurveda' is traditional Hindu wisdom bringing mind-body balance. Indians have known for a long time about the value of spices and their Ayurvedic properties and how the different flavours affect the person. Cooking at home becomes essential in contributing to family life and general wellbeing. The mother in the family is in power in the kitchen, nurturing her extended family with great love. When produce is homegrown, this love is extended even further whilst sustaining the growth of the produce. A similar relationship is observed when the male members of the family go fishing and proudly display their catch, providing a meal for loved ones. In restaurants, such emotions can exist when the chef or restaurateur feels they have truly nourished their clients.

In the West, chilli is perhaps the spice usually connected with Indian food. Chillies are used in India, particularly in the South whether fresh, pickled, dried or ground. It was actually the Portuguese who brought chilli to India at the beginning of the fifteenth century. Chilli was encountered by European explorers in the Caribbean and introduced to their homelands. In India, prior to the introduction of chilli, pepper was the spice which gave heat to food. Despite Indians being slow to accept new foodstuffs, chillies quickly became an essential ingredient in South Indian cuisine. Ayurvedic physicians, who rarely used foreign foods, replaced pepper with chillies in some of their remedies. Chillies were cheap, so used to provide taste to a meal of rice and lentils as well as a vital source of vitamin C. Present-day South Indian cooking is heavy-handed in the use of chillies. The sauces of curry in the South are thick with a sour flavouring derived from tamarind, which was introduced into India from Africa by Arab traders; coconut is also used as a base for many sauces.

The Portuguese introduced confectionary to Goa, including desserts made with milk that took a distinct Indian flavour with the use of coconut milk and spices like cardamom. The Goans incorporated coconut milk and tamarind to create a truly fusion cuisine experience. The most famous of all Goan dishes is vindaloo, now making its presence in most Indian restaurants. Vindaloo is actually a Goan adaptation of a Portuguese dish, which was cooked in wine, vinegar and garlic.

Anglo-Indian cuisine adopted techniques and ingredients from each region to create hybrid dishes. The British introduced some European vegetables such as pumpkin and cabbage to India. The Indian cooking style however remained unchanged. The mainly vegetarian population now had a wider selection of vegetables. One of the most important food commodities introduced to the Indians by the British would be tea. Cha, which is the Chinese word for tea, was included in the language as 'chai'. India today is one of the largest tea producers and consumers.

In Britain, curries were originally meals associated with the upper classes. The meals did reach the middle-class, progressing eventually to the working-class homes. In modern times, curry is popular in many restaurants and takeaways, homes and pubs with the popular 'curry nights'. The variety of vegetarian options makes these restaurants attractive and welcoming to vegetarians. Tandoori restaurants with imported clay ovens emerged in the 1970s. Exclusive restaurants serve versions of curry along with quality wines. The first of such restaurants was Veeraswamy's which opened in 1926 and remains the opulent landmark today.

Food writer, television chef and entrepreneur, Madhur Jaffrey's books and television shows helped immensely in getting the British to experience another culture and discover what curries were about. Dressed in gorgeous sarees, she cooked in attractive locations and her preparation of simple recipes made her very accessible to the community.

Foods such as chicken tikka masala are now considered a British national dish, this showing the British acceptance of international influences and including them in their eating habits, exemplifying a multicultural Britain. The popularity of curries can be due to many factors such as the availability of Indian ingredients and increased immigration after the Second World War, with many immigrants engaged in restaurants. Another contributing factor could be nostalgia due to the historical ties. No doubt curries add a thrill to bland, traditional British food.

Indian cuisine has not lost its identity despite the various influences. It has gained more flavour, depth and diversity whilst maintaining the main principle of purity and balance. Central to Indian cuisine are onions, garlic, ginger and spices such as cardamom, clove, fennel and turmeric which are known to have therapeutic properties. Meals are served as a banquet rather than as numerous courses. Savouries may be eaten prior to the main meal otherwise they accompany the meal. Indian bread will be used to gather curries and accompaniments and savouring the sauces. Dhal may be taken with rice and remaining or additional serves of curries. Traditionally, food is eaten with the tips of the fingers although cutlery is introduced for some dishes such as dhal in some homes.

WHAT *IS* CURRY?

The idea of a 'curry' is a British concept, based on the Tamil word *kari* which refers to black pepper. The term is used to represent a variety of Indian dishes, especially those foods prepared in sauces. Indians referred to their dishes by specific names depending on the spice potpourri e.g. rogan josh, cooking method e.g. korma or the main ingredient such as aloo gobi for a cauliflower dish. The British categorised dishes such as rogan josh and dopiaza as 'curry', a term they learned from the Portuguese, who had introduced these terms from words in South Indian languages.

Defining curry is elusive. In this book, it is a term for individual meals such as a spicy dish of meat, seafood or vegetable, often served in a sauce, accompanied by rice or rice dishes and or wheat-based breads or an entire cuisine or food culture. The use of spices and other flavours such as garlic and onion give Indian cuisine a distinct quality.

I can recall being told when I first came to reside in New Zealand in the 1970s that leftover Sunday roast was made into curry a day or two later as spices livened up the meat. This was quite a revelation and disconcerting to me, knowing well how valued curry from a freshly slaughtered goat or chicken was in Fiji. The idea of using cold meat cooked with onions and chilli in this way is the origin of jalfrezi in Britain. The irony here is that eating of leftovers was taboo amongst many Hindus.

Nineteenth-century English novelist, W. M. Thackeray acquired a taste for curries in the homes of his aunts and uncles who had lived in India. Thackeray was born in India but was sent home at the age of four to receive an education, a practice that was not uncommon. He wrote the following poem, inspired by his interest in curries (Punch, or The London Charivari, 1846, p. 221).

Kitchen Melodies - Curry

THREE pounds of veal my darling girl prepares,
And chops it nicely into little squares;
Five onions next prures the little minx
(The biggest are the best, her SAMIWEL thinks).
And Epping butter nearly half-a-pound,
And stews them in a pan until they're brown'd.

What's next my dextrous little girl will do?
She pops the meat into the savoury stew,
With curry-powder table-spoonfuls three,
And milk a pint, (the richest that may be)
And, when the dish has stewed for half-an hour,
A lemon's ready juice she'll o'er it pour:
Then, bless her! then she gives the luscious pot
A very gentle boil – and serves quite hot.

P.S. - Beef, mutton, rabbit, if you wish;
Lobsters, or prawns, or any kind fish
Are fit to make A CURRY. 'Tis when done,
A dish for Emperors to feed upon.

IN INDIA

In North India, a typical meal would consist of paratha (wholewheat bread) sometimes stuffed with potato (aloo paratha), served with vegetables and/or meat with creamy yoghurt and pickles. Other options include channa bhatura (deep-fried bread with chickpeas). Lassi is a yoghurt-based drink flavoured with fruit such as mango, or simply salted; and chai is a favourite at any time of the day.

Dosa is popular in all meals in South India. It is a light pancake made from a fermented batter of rice and lentils. A tantalising combination of coconut, garlic, onions, chillies, curry leaves and fried black mustard seeds is an accompaniment with a fiery, hot sambhaar (spicy lentil soup). Vegetables and at times meat curries would accompany the meal. Masala dosa (spicy potato filled dosa) is becoming a favourite with Australians who have been introduced to South Indian cuisine. Also popular are idlis having similar ingredients to dosa but steamed until soft and puffy.

There are some key tastes in South Indian cuisine. These are sweet (milk, butter or ghee, sugar or jaggery); sour (citrus, mango or tamarind); salty (salt or pickles); bitter (bitter gourd, fenugreek or turmeric); and astringent (lentils, coriander and vegetables such as cabbage or cauliflower).

Indians do not normally consume alcohol with meals; they drink first then sit down to a meal. Food habits like most aspects of the Indian lifestyle have undergone changes and middle-class Indians are known to indulge in wine with their meals, both imported and locally produced. Local vineyards are known to be producing premium wines, some of which are exported.

In restaurants, thali meals are served on a banana leaf or stainless-steel platter with rice or roti and curries (vegetarian or non-vegetarian), dhal or sambhaar, curds and pickles.

INDIANS IN FIJI

The prominent Indian settlement in the Pacific we see today started in 1879. Approximately 60,000 Indians landed in Fiji between 1879 and 1916. They came as indentured labourers. The reasons for their decision to come to Fiji were economic and to escape the insecure future of their birth place. The migrants were mostly young, between twenty to thirty years of age, and were excited by the promise of a land of opportunities offered by the recruiters. Their perception of Fiji or their work was often vague and the ability to work and accumulate wealth in order to return to the homeland was attractive. It wasn't until the Gujerati immigration around 1920 that Indians engaged in commercial enterprise.

The Indian labourers soon found that life was tough with illness, ill treatment, rudimentary living conditions and long hours of toil. Most stayed, creating a form of Indian society with their unique food sensation. Indians speaking different dialects co-existed, bringing an ambitious and motivated presence to the Pacific.

The unique blend in Indian cuisine we see today in Fiji is a legacy of their ancestors. This food has been transported to places such as Australia, New Zealand, Canada, US and the UK wherever Fiji Indians have emigrated to over the decades.

MY HOME

Certain foods evoke memories of childhood, a ritualistic Sunday lunch consisting of a trip to the market to procure fish for a hearty fish curry delivered to an assembled audience. Prior to cooking, fish was soaked in tamarind water to add the sour flavour as fish was seen to match well with tamarind. Being connoisseurs, the quality of the produce and comparison with other similar dining experiences would be a topic of conversation for my parents. On some occasions, we would be fortunate enough to include fish which the family, particularly Dad and my brother, had brought home after a fishing trip. The fishing trip had an early start with special foods for lunch prepared for the hopeful 'fishermen' accompanied by the obligatory Fijian beer. Mum would eagerly await their return and be overjoyed if her favourite fish was in the catch. Amidst the excitement and competitiveness, the actual fishing was a solemn occasion especially for my brother, Bimal, who was an earnest fisherman at all times. Having spent part of his childhood on the smaller islands, Dad had an affinity with anything to do with the sea.

The Fiji Indian curries differ in taste and texture from curries of India. In Fiji Indian curries oil, onion, ginger, garlic, chilli, turmeric, curry powder, cardamom, cumin, cloves and cinnamon are the base ingredients, whereas in India the richness of the sauces is obtained from tomatoes, coconut milk and yoghurts. In some homes, the cooking style of India was adhered to on special occasions.

In Fiji, the dishes are influenced by one's origin in India. Whilst the Indians have adopted wheat as well as rice into their diet, there remain some regional flavours and cooking styles. The flavours and choice of ingredients reflect a Northern or Southern influence. North Indian curries are dominant in Fiji although South Indian cuisine has become increasingly popular. The spiciness and generous use of chilli by Fiji's South Indians continues to give their food a distinct flavour. I learned to prepare such dishes under the watchful eye of Mum and along the way, acquired a love of cooking. As I entertain today, I constantly assess my efforts and feel Mum's presence in my kitchen.

I wonder if my dishes would gain her approval and how she would have improvised on methodology and choice of ingredients. Upon reflecting on the many influences in my cooking, my childhood experience, interests acquired in the Western countries I have resided in and collaboration with friends are some that stand out. Ultimately, each home develops a particular style of cooking and so food has varied flavours from one home to another.

I have memories of Mum buying spices, washing and cleaning them to dry in the sun for hours before grinding them. The grinding task was later adopted by Indian grocery shops. Nowadays curry powder, a mixture of spices also known as masala, is bought from Indian grocery shops. These are often supplemented with freshly ground spices. Convenient mixtures can be obtained for fish or meat curries. The argument for not using pre-prepared mixtures is the different length of time spices take to release flavour. Coriander releases flavour more slowly than turmeric and needs to be added to oil prior to turmeric. The way a spice is treated before it is added to the dish determines the flavour of the spice. When spices are fried, they tend to be more aromatic than if they are added to a sauce. To top meat curries with curry leaves allows for a slow release of flavour in contrast to frying the leaves with spices.

Traditional kitchen gadgets were used for tasks such as blending and scraping coconut. Chillies and herbs for chutneys or soaked dhal for savouries were initially made into a paste using sil and lora or curry stone; naturally the stone gradually transitioned to pestle and mortar made in stone or marble and to electrical appliances.

In Fiji, there is a keen sense of hospitality and entertaining and this was certainly the case in my home. Mum enjoyed making hot rotis for appreciative guests even if it meant working in sweltering conditions; painstaking it may have been but for Mum a pleasurable experience all around. The meal she had conjured with immense finesse was presented with a wide selection of enticing food. Mum would go out of her way to cook each guest's favourite dish, which was invariably appreciated with gusto often surpassing expectations. Food and drink would be pressed upon all from arrival to departure. If unexpected guests were to arrive, Mum would be quick to accommodate them with easily prepared delicacies such as mouth-watering bhajias or pakoras, which are deep-fried vegetables in spiced chickpea batter. Indians expect to be force-fed when they visit others, enjoying the attention given to them. Indians of my grandparents' generation would think it rude and are disappointed if the host does not force-feed them.

Westerners are not accustomed to this treatment. This was a lesson I learned promptly when I first arrived in Auckland at the age of sixteen. Because it was polite to refuse food when first offered, I did so waiting for the offer to be repeated. It did not take me long to adapt to the local habits. It was also challenging to respond to questions such as 'What would you like to eat?' as the expectation would have been that the meal would be simply served with numerous dishes to select from.

When I glance at Mum's recipe books with her special repertoire of dishes – turmeric-stained or splattered with some cake mixture – I am reminded of the love in these little treasures as they stand out amongst cookery books from noteworthy writers and chefs. At times, the measurements used depended on the receptacle the particular ingredient was purchased in such as a condensed milk tin being used as a measure. Expertise on measures was gained through observations, practice and judgements. I also find useful comments and advice at the end of recipes, offering substitutions for ingredients. I like to imagine when I am preparing for a dinner party that the activities and aromas of my kitchen transform it into Mum's.

FIJI INDIAN CUISINE

Fiji Indian food is a mixture of Indian, Melanesian, Polynesian, Chinese and Western cuisine. It is home-style, unpretentious cooking filled with flavours. Indians came to Fiji approximately 130 years ago and have had the biggest influence on food in Fiji. The spectacular markets cater for all ethnic groups. Restaurants offer a hybrid cuisine inviting all communities to partake in satisfying a common culinary pleasure or need. Fiji Indian style of cooking is common in the kitchens of the island's top resorts. Buffets of considerable panache consisting of Indian, Fijian, Chinese and Western meals are typically displayed in hotel dining rooms throughout Fiji.

Although many Indians have not travelled to or have any connection with relatives in India, the influences of the motherland in religion, traditions and cuisine are very much alive in Fiji.

In the early days, Indians were forced to adapt their cooking to ingredients available locally, creating a distinctive style. When the Gujarati traders arrived, they brought clothes, jewellery and spices. Indian food has travelled nicely to Fiji with the indentured labourers. Indians buy Fijian root crops such as taro or dalo and eat them boiled or boiled and fried in a chickpea batter. Indians have preserved their eating habits and Fijians find it hard to resist a curry. A very popular island vegetable, roro (leaves of the taro plant), has been incorporated into the Indian diet. Saina is a celebrated savoury made by rubbing the taro leaves with lemon juice and spreading a spicy chickpea mixture on the leaves. This is rolled, steamed, sliced and fried resulting in an irresistible treat.

Coconuts are a common and desirable ingredient in the islands. The process of producing coconut cream for consistency and flavour is an interesting experience. Coconut cream is made by grating the coconut flesh with a hand grater or food processor. A cup of warm water is mixed with a cup of coconut meat and this mixture is stirred and squeezed or placed in a food processor on high until combined. The mixture is then sieved.

To make coconut milk, the above process is repeated by adding two cups of water for every cup of coconut meat. Both the cream and milk can be frozen. Because they will solidify in the freezer, before use, the mixture needs to be thawed and whisked. Coconut oil is used in cooking and the juice provides a refreshing beverage.

Fijian foods show Indian influences in their adoption of spices and herbs. A Fiji favourite, kakoda (raw fish marinated in coconut cream), is sometimes prepared with seasoning such as onions and fresh chillies garnished with fresh coriander borrowed from Indian cuisine. A Fijian feast reserved for special occasions is a lovu which is relished by Fijians and many Indians. The lovu is created by digging a large hole in the ground. A fire is created to heat the stones and when the flames subside, meats wrapped in banana leaves are placed in the pit. Everything is covered with more banana leaves and hot stones and left to cook for hours. These days, some of the meat will be marinated with spices to encapsulate the flavours before they make their way into the pit. Indian food such as roti wrap (Indian bread filled with meat or vegetable curry spiked with pickle and sold in food stalls) is keenly devoured by some Fijian school children who find this a desirable alternative to their traditional food. Tinned fish curry is another popular meal.

Chinese food has not escaped Indian influence. Chicken cubes tossed in a concoction of soy sauce and spices is a favourite fusion dish. Indian Chinese food came about when Chinese immigrants settled in present-day Kolkata, adapting to the local preferences for spicy food; the cuisine is now popular globally. Chilli and cumin give the food the kick that is favoured. Indian Chinese restaurants are sprouting in Sydney where a dish of fried rice may be served with spices galore. Some of the popular spices used are peppercorns, coriander and dry chillies; likewise in Fiji.

Through the University of the South Pacific, Indian food has spread to other parts of the Pacific. In the early days of the university canteen, there was a section for Indian students serving rice, roti, dhal, meat and vegetables whilst the island section served boiled root crops, beef and pork. Gradually the students started to experiment with other food types and Indian food gained popularity. On islands other than Fiji where there has been no history of Indian immigration, one can find tins of curry powder. In Samoa, curried tinned fish and beef are relished together with root vegetables such as taro, with more Indian dishes appearing commercially.

ECLECTIC INSPIRATIONS

The tantalising allure of Indian cuisine has found its way in the West very successfully making the eating experience truly eclectic. The adapting and adopting of ingredients and cooking styles have given rise to a fusion of culinary styles, which is relished in the West and appreciated by many. The ubiquitous curry influence has travelled far.

Some friends who initially resisted or found the aromas of Indian spices and herbs such as coriander overpowering, gradually attuned to curries as part of their dining experience. Once they were assimilated, they couldn't have enough of curries.

There were some limitations with Indian cooking due to available ingredients in New Zealand when my family emigrated there. However, this has changed rapidly over the years to the extent that Fijian fish and mangoes can grace a dinner table in New Zealand with numerous supermarkets selling a gamut of items from groceries, fresh produce to sweets and home-cooked meals. There is a strong Bangladeshi influence in restaurants in Britain whilst Punjabi cuisine dominates Australian restaurants. South Indian cuisine has been introduced in Australia by Indians, Sri Lankans, Malaysians and Singaporeans presenting regional cuisine from the South. More and more restaurants are serving under 'Goan' or 'Keralan' regional cuisines and this trend could continue to include more varieties. Australia has a very diverse food culture with many Australians fancying Asian meals in restaurants and homes.

In frequenting restaurants, one observes different ways of eating e.g. seasoned disc-shaped snacks known as pappadums (or pappad as they are often called in Fiji) and pickles with yoghurt dressing would normally be eaten with the main meal; however, in restaurants these can be served as starters. This developed from the European expectation that meals should be divided into courses. Restaurants introduced tandoor ovens – a popular innovation, even though nearly all of the Indian homes would not possess one. Tandoors provide a theatrical experience as they are often visible from the dining area.

Many Indian restaurants will use shortcuts to meal preparation as these are quick, easy and reasonably priced. The curry sauces are prepared in advance and meat pre-cooked. Use of pre-packaged spices, food colouring and flavour enhancers are not uncommon. Diners can expect a standardisation, so some food, such as samosas, in many restaurants, have the same flavouring as they have been sourced from a common supplier. I am intrigued at the reverence bestowed on butter chicken, a dish made more palatable to Western taste and considered by some as the epitome of fine Indian food. This is because I was introduced to the dish after leaving Fiji and found when I arrived in Australia that it had already gained considerable favour. To some Indians, the curries served in restaurants are not authentic.

Cooking has been simplified in many ways to accommodate our busy lifestyle. Butchers marinate meat with spicy sauces whilst pre-prepared curries can be bought in bags to be heated and served. Meat can be simmered in ready-made sauces.

Western and Indian food is tempered with authenticity whilst mixing bits of this and that. The result is interesting. The food is the result of two cultures being thrown together evolving into a unique cultural hotpot with resemblance to Indian cooking. Lasagna with paneer or cottage cheese is such an example. Curry sauces are flavoured with chips and a particular favourite with my children was toast with curry sauces. The answer to Caesar salad can be a vegetarian Gandhi salad with a combination of lettuce, tomato, cucumber, Spanish onion and cottage cheese. Western curries using raisins or apples are not so common nowadays with the increased familiarity with Indian food. The use of ingredients not commonly used in Indian cuisine can be welcomed in certain dishes. For instance, I supplement my avocado chutney and pakoras with a combination of herbs including dill, a herb generally associated with Scandinavian fish and lamb dishes.

With Indians travelling within their country, regional cuisines have seen some merging. All this taking place in a country where there was a pronounced distinction between regions with even chapattis being made differently in areas consuming them.

With globalisation and the demand for Indian spices in the West, crops that are not economic may no longer be produced. The following generations will not have the knowledge of abundance of flavours of, say, bananas in Kerala in India's South.

To appreciate cuisine, it is vital to understand that all cuisines cross borders. Explorers brought back to their country of origin what they liked on their travels.

French, Italian and Spanish cuisines are a result of these explorations. Ingredients from all over the world can be cooked and served in harmony. Improvisation can be done adequately so coconut milk instead of cream can be used in a baked custard. The flavour and texture are altered tastefully.

There are foods that are truly universal. Yoghurt and curd dishes have travelled extensively in some form or other, being consumed daily in countries like India and Russia and gaining favour with newer converts like China. In India, yoghurt is thought to aid in digestion. It is used in the preparation of many dishes and eaten as is or flavoured with salt or sugar.

The food of the Raj had some creative influences such as seen in kedgere, a breakfast dish combining rice, smoked fish, boiled eggs and spices. It is derived from khicheri which is a boiled mixture of rice and lentils lightly flavoured with turmeric. Another adaptation is mulligatawny soup from the South Indian rasam, a soup of lentils and spices. Mulligatawny translates to pepper or chilli water, which are the components of the dish. To this the British added meat or vegetables and flour to thicken. Shepherd's pie would be served with a flavouring of cumin and topped with sesame seeds.

This blend of spices was an attempt by the Europeans to replicate their memory of Indian cuisine. The Europeans took curry everywhere, making it a truly global dish, thus we find goat curry in Jamaica, Japanese curry, fish cake in Iceland enhanced with a dash of cumin and the popular fast-food, German currywurst – pork sausage with a sprinkle of curry powder and topped with tomato sauce. In South-East Asian countries, curries are an integral part of the cuisine. Such popularity makes curries an extraordinary food. It appears that commercial curry powder has been in existence since the 1780s.

Whilst classical dishes with traditional ingredients are worthy of their credit, cooking is a living art which is prone to change and development. There will be some who lament the changes and continue to remain true to the cooking of their parents and grandparents as in some homes fads are not so common and many dishes remain unchanged.

Changes are however inevitable as the art of cookery is not sacrosanct. Using ingenuity and prowess, techniques can be adapted, new ingredients introduced and old recipes revived. The generation my children belong to will bring more influences and perhaps shortcuts to the dishes they will select to be in their repertoire. Cookbooks have experienced a change – they include more than cooking ingredients and techniques. There is an acknowledgement of a lifestyle related to eating amidst the cultural, historical and spiritual influences. Whilst being guided by recipes, even simple ones, the breaks in food preparation allow us to have pauses we precisely need – time for reflection, improvements or simply a well-earned rest from a frenzied and sometimes overwhelming lifestyle.

As I contemplate the sharing of food, I am absolutely convinced that we must find time for restorative meals with those we care about. This must extend to the wider community as we interact, forming harmonious relationships with those belonging to diverse cultures.

FESTIVALS

Of all the festivals we were accustomed to, Diwali, which is known as the festival of lights, celebrated by Hindus, was the one most widely celebrated in Fiji. Candles, lamps and later, electric lights displayed a brilliant sight. There were fireworks and of course the mandatory visitations to friends and relatives to savour the rich, often milky and beautifully flavoured sweets. We would recollect which families prepared the tastiest of our favourite sweets and anticipated the gifts.

The festival occurs in October or November and lasts for a few days. Prior to the celebration, there is much activity in homes with the preparation of sweets to share. Popular sweets on the occasion are barfi, laddoo and gulab jamun.

The Muslim community celebrated Eid al-Fitr marking the end of the month-long fast of Ramadan. Here you could be expected to be treated to a hearty goat pulau and sweets such as sewai. We delighted in sharing meals with our Muslim friends on such occasions.

RECIPES

The criteria for selection of recipes are their popularity with family and friends; easy to prepare, yet tasty and mostly inspirations from Mum with a few from relatives and family friends. There are a few recipes that would require perseverance and practice to perfect such as tamarind chutney, the breads and desserts such as payasam and ladoo. Many of them are simple, so the cook is not overwhelmed and can be creative and adventurous.

I see my recipes as a starting point with suggestions, not necessarily about having a precise set of ingredients and instructions. If preference is for particular tastes, then add more or less of the particular ingredient, such as more chillies for a vibrant curry, less fenugreek if bitterness is not preferred in a vegetable dish. Tasting as you cook is obligatory to refine your dishes.

For ingredients, I have adhered to English names except when none were available. Some ingredients commonly known by Hindi names such as ghee for clarified butter have been listed as such. Lentils and a few other ingredients specifically labelled with Hindi names in the respective grocery shops have both English and Hindi names.

As an oven guide, for fan-forced ovens, the oven temperature can be set to 20°C lower than the recipe instruction.

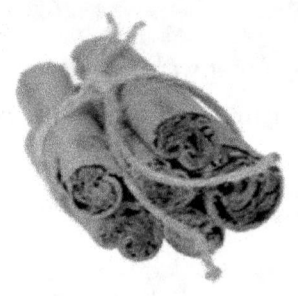

SNACKS/ENTRÉE

Dhokla

Steamed, lightly spiced, fluffy snack.

SERVES 6

- 1 cup coarse semolina
- 1 cup yoghurt
- 1 dessertspoon desiccated coconut
- ½ cup chopped onion
- ½ cup grated carrot
- ½ cup shredded cabbage (optional)
- 1 teaspoon fruit salt or 1 teaspoon each of baking powder and baking soda
- 1 tablespoon chickpea flour (besan)
- ½ teaspoon crushed ginger
- 1 clove crushed garlic
- 3 dessertspoons oil
- ½ teaspoon mustard seeds
- 1 teaspoon sesame seeds
- ½ teaspoon turmeric
- ½ teaspoon salt
- ¼ teaspoon chilli powder
- 2 tablespoons chopped coriander leaves

Mix all ingredients, place in oiled baking tin, cover with foil and steam in a steamer for approximately 30 minutes. Heat oil, add mustard and sesame seeds. Pour over steamed dhokla. Serve with coconut or tamarind chutney as an entrée or with tea.

Bhajia or Pakora

Bhajia is the common name in Fiji for this very popular savoury consisting of vegetables in chickpea flour batter which are deep-fried into crunchy balls.

MAKES APPROXIMATELY 20–25

- 1 cup chickpea flour (besan)
- 1 teaspoon sesame seeds
- 1 cup vegetables (shredded cabbage plus carrot)
- 2 tablespoons chopped coriander leaves
- ½ cup chopped onion
- 1 clove crushed garlic
- ½ teaspoon baking powder
- 6 chopped curry leaves
- ½ teaspoon crushed ginger
- 1 teaspoon cumin seeds
- 1 teaspoon salt
- ½ teaspoon chilli powder
- ½ teaspoon fennel seeds
- Oil for deep frying

Mix all ingredients and leave for an hour. If required, add drops of water to achieve thick batter consistency. Make into small balls and deep fry until golden brown. Bhajia is best served warm when it is crunchy and is fine on its own or with a chilli or tamarind chutney.

VARIATIONS

Silverbeet or spinach and grated potato can be substituted for cabbage and carrot. For a change, to ½ cup chickpea flour add ½ cup of self-raising flour and omit baking powder.

Seafood Pakora

An interesting variation on vegetable pakoras to tickle your taste buds, one of the recipes accredited to Aunty Ratna.

MAKES APPROXIMATELY 20

- 1 cup self-raising flour
- 300g diced fish fillet (snapper) or prawns
- 1 tablespoon chopped coriander leaves
- ½ teaspoon salt
- ½ cup chopped onion
- ½ teaspoon chilli powder
- 2 cloves crushed garlic
- Oil for deep frying
- 1 teaspoon cumin seeds

Mix all ingredients, make small balls and deep fry. Serve hot with coconut or tamarind chutney.

Samosa

Vegetable-filled, deep-fried, crispy and golden parcel. Vegetables can be substituted for meat, both are popular.

MAKES 30 SAMOSAS

- 4 tablespoons oil, additional for deep frying
- 1 ½ teaspoons curry powder
- 2 teaspoons turmeric (optional)
- 6 medium sized potatoes
- 2 cups peas (frozen or soak dried peas overnight and boil for 45 minutes)
- 3 cloves crushed garlic
- 6–10 chopped curry leaves (optional)
- ½ teaspoon mustard seeds
- 1 ½ teaspoons salt
- 2 chopped fresh chilli (or ½ teaspoon chilli powder)
- Juice of 1 small lemon
- ½ teaspoon crushed ginger
- ½ teaspoon fenugreek seeds
- ½ teaspoon cumin seeds
- 2 tablespoons chopped coriander leaves
- 1 packet with 20 spring roll pastry sheets

Heat oil, add curry leaves, fenugreek, mustard and cumin seeds. Add ginger, garlic, chilli, turmeric, curry powder and salt. Add potatoes and peas (if frozen, add when potatoes are almost cooked) and fry until vegetables are cooked. Add salt and mix in lemon juice and chopped coriander leaves.

Thaw and cut spring roll pastry sheets into 3 lengths. For each samosa use a double sheet. Place 2 teaspoons of mixture at the end of 1 sheet and fold over to make a triangle shape. Continue until you come to the end of the pastry. Seal with water and deep fry until golden brown. Drain off excess oil and serve hot with tamarind chutney.

Spring roll pastry is easy to work with; roti recipe is the traditional use. After rolling the roti dough, cut in half, fold and fill the pockets, pressing down on the sides with a fork. See steps for samosa made with prepared roti dough.

VARIATIONS

Substitute frozen peas with cauliflower or shredded cabbage. Shortcrust pastry can be substituted for spring roll pastry. The ends can be brushed with egg mixture and samosas baked for 25–30 minutes.

For meat samosa, all vegetables except potato can be substituted for ½ kilogram of minced lamb, omit turmeric and double the quantity of curry powder, ginger and garlic.

Saina

Taro leaves with seasoned chickpea flour paste, steamed and deep-fried.

MAKES APPROXIMATELY 24 PIECES WITH LARGE LEAVES

- 12–15 taro leaves (or silverbeet with the broad stalks trimmed)
- 1 teaspoon cumin seeds
- 1 teaspoon fennel seeds
- 2 cups chickpea flour (besan), additional for paste when frying
- Oil for frying
- 2 teaspoons crushed ginger
- 2 large cloves crushed garlic
- 1 chopped chilli
- Juice of 4 lemons
- 1 teaspoon salt
- 1 teaspoon curry powder

Cover leaves with lemon juice. Mix all ingredients (except oil) and spread paste on underside of leaves, make piles of 6–7 leaves. Roll like a spring roll (fold top, then sides and roll). Wrap in aluminium foil and steam in a steamer for 5-10 minutes. With remaining chickpea flour, add water to make a paste. Slice thinly, dip in chickpea flour paste and fry.

VARIATIONS

Alternatively, after steaming rolls, slice and fry in oil with sesame and mustard seeds and enjoy as a snack. I use chickpea flour although black lentil (urad dhal) flour is very suitable and easier to spread.

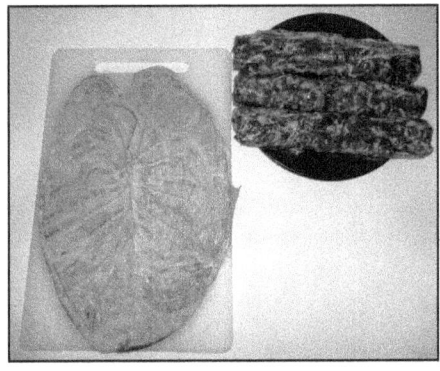

Nimki

Crunchy, deep-fried tea snack from Aunty Sudha.

MAKES APPROXIMATELY 40–50

2 cups plain flour
1 tablespoon cornflour
¼ teaspoon turmeric
1 heaped tablespoon baking powder
1 teaspoon cumin seeds
1 teaspoon sesame seeds
1 tablespoon butter
1 teaspoon salt
½ teaspoon chilli powder
½ teaspoon caster sugar
Oil for deep frying

Mix all dry ingredients together. Rub in butter. Make into a dough with cold water. Dough is to be slightly firmer than roti dough. Roll out and cut into small triangles and leave for ½ an hour. Fry in hot oil over low heat. Nimki can be kept in air-tight containers for days and is a popular Diwali treat.

Upmao

Semolina-based South Indian snack or breakfast.

SERVES 4–6

- 1 cup coarse semolina
- 2 cups water
- ½ cup vegetables (carrot, beans, peas or zucchini)
- 1 teaspoon salt
- ¼ cup chopped peanuts or almonds
- 3 dessertspoons ghee or olive oil
- 8 curry leaves
- ½ teaspoon crushed ginger
- ½ cup chopped onion
- ½ teaspoon chilli powder
- ½ teaspoon mustard seeds
- 2 dessertspoons lemon juice

Dry roast semolina or fry in ghee. Fry onion, vegetables, peanuts, curry leaves, ginger, chilli, mustard seeds and salt in ghee. Add semolina and water and lastly lemon juice.

Corn fritters

I adore this snack even now, scrutinising breakfast menus for this favourite from my childhood.

SERVES 10–12

- 1 cup flour
- 2 teaspoons baking powder
- 1 egg
- ½ teaspoon salt
- 2 heaped tablespoons chopped coriander leaves or chives
- 2 cups creamed corn or kernels
- ½ – ¾ cup milk (lesser amount required with creamed corn)
- ½ chopped onion
- 1 tablespoon melted butter
- ½ teaspoon paprika
- Pepper to taste
- Oil for frying

Sift flour and baking powder. Whisk egg and add milk, mix into flour mixture. Add other ingredients and shallow-fry 1 tablespoon at a time in pan until golden, cooking both sides. Serve hot with a chutney or chilli sauce. Ideal for breakfast or as a snack.

Kakoda

Fijian raw fish – tangy and creamy.

SERVES 4–6

- 750g fish (snapper or mullet)
- 1 cup lemon or lime juice
- Coconut milk from 1 coconut or 1 cup thick coconut cream
- 1 teaspoon salt
- 1 chopped chilli
- Tomato or shallots for garnish
- Chopped coriander leaves

Cut fish fillets into 1cm pieces. Sprinkle with salt and leave for a few minutes. Pour lemon juice over fish – the fish must be just covered by juice. Leave for 2–3 hours or overnight in the refrigerator until the fish is white. (The time taken to 'whiten' depends on the kind of fish and the acidity of the lemons or limes. Cooling slows down the process). Strain off juice and squeeze out moisture by pressing in a strainer.

Pour coconut cream over the fish. Add chilli and coriander leaves. Garnish with chopped shallots or tomato. Serve well chilled.

Other variations for savouries:

Root vegetables such as boiled tapioca (cassava) or boiled taro as well as potatoes and eggplants can be sliced and dipped in a chickpea flour batter with a pinch of chilli and salt and deep-fried. This is a popular afternoon or pre-dinner snack.

Using a fondue set or kadai (round Indian frying pan), I have prepared a concoction using a commercial balti sauce. To the balti sauce I add chopped tomatoes and yoghurt to be served with savoury puris, crackers or a vegetable platter.

MEAT / FISH / EGG

Egg Curry

SERVES 4

- 4 boiled eggs with eggshells removed
- 1 chopped boiled potato
- 1 small sliced onion
- ½ cup tomato paste
- ½ cup coconut milk
- 4 tablespoons oil
- ½ teaspoon crushed garlic
- 1 teaspoon turmeric
- 1 teaspoon curry powder
- 1 teaspoon mustard seeds
- ½ teaspoon cumin seeds
- ½ teaspoon fenugreek seeds
- 1 teaspoon salt
- 1 whole chilli
- 1 tablespoon chopped coriander leaves

Heat oil and sear eggs, put aside. In the remaining oil, fry onion with mustard, cumin and fenugreek seeds. Add garlic, salt and chilli and powdered spices cooking until onion is lightly browned. Mix in tomato paste and coconut milk and stir well, then add eggs and potatoes. Stir through coriander leaves before serving.

Pulau

Fragrant basmati rice with spicy meat. A festive dish.

SERVES 6–8

- 1kg diced lamb, goat or chicken
- 1 chopped onion
- 2 teaspoons crushed ginger
- 4 cloves crushed garlic
- 6 whole cardamom
- 1 cinnamon stick
- 6 cloves
- 2–3 star anise
- 1 teaspoon cumin seeds
- 1 teaspoon fennel seeds
- 1 dessertspoon garam masala
- 1 teaspoon coriander seeds
- 2 dessertspoons curry powder
- 8–10 curry leaves
- 2 dessertspoons soy sauce
- 2 grated carrots
- 1 dessertspoon salt
- 3 cups cooked basmati rice
- 2 tablespoons ghee or olive oil

Heat ghee, add spices then ginger and garlic, garam masala, curry powder, meat, soy sauce and carrots. When meat is cooked, add rice. Pulau goes well with raita.

This simple version uses cooked rice whereas a traditional one simmers rice and meat together requiring precision in timing and water quantity.

Chicken Curry

SERVES 6

- 500g diced chicken
- 4 dessertspoons oil
- 1 chopped onion
- 2 teaspoons crushed ginger
- 4 cloves crushed garlic
- 1 dessertspoon turmeric
- 1 teaspoon mustard seeds
- 4 whole cardamom
- 6 curry leaves
- 1 teaspoon fenugreek seeds
- 1 teaspoon cumin seeds
- 2 dessertspoons curry powder
- ½ dessertspoon garam masala
- 2 tablespoons tomato paste
- 2 teaspoons salt
- 2 dessertspoons chopped coriander

Heat oil, add onion and spices and cook until onion is browned. Add ginger, garlic, turmeric, curry powder, garam masala, tomato paste and meat. Add salt and coriander when meat is cooked. Serve with rice or your favourite bread.

VARIATION

For a tomato-rich curry, add 300g each of chopped tomatoes and onions in the sauce and simmer until sauce thickens. Add chicken to simmering sauce and when cooked, add salt and coriander leaves.

Lamb Curry

SERVES 4

- 500g diced lamb
- 4 dessertspoons oil
- 1 chopped onion
- 2 teaspoons crushed ginger
- 4 cloves crushed garlic
- 1 cinnamon stick
- 1 teaspoon mustard seeds
- 1 teaspoon cumin seeds
- 1 dessertspoon turmeric
- 1 ½ dessertspoons curry powder
- 1 dessertspoon garam masala
- 3 chopped medium tomatoes
- 2 teaspoons salt
- 2 dessertspoons chopped coriander leaves
- 6–8 curry leaves

Heat oil, add onion, curry leaves and spices and cook until onion is browned. Add ginger, garlic, turmeric, curry powder, garam masala and meat and after 10 minutes, add tomatoes. Mix in salt and coriander when meat is cooked. Serve with rice or bread.

VARIATION

Omit turmeric for a wonderfully spiced tomato lamb dish.

Fish Curry

SERVES 4

- 500g snapper cut into fillets
- 4 tablespoons tamarind pulp or juice of 1 lemon
- 8 curry leaves
- 4 dessertspoons oil
- 1 chopped onion
- 2 teaspoons crushed ginger
- 4 cloves crushed garlic
- 2 teaspoons salt
- 1 teaspoon combined cumin, fenugreek and mustard seeds
- ¼ teaspoon chilli powder
- 2 dessertspoons curry powder
- 2 teaspoons turmeric
- 2 dessertspoons tomato paste
- 2 dessertspoons chopped coriander leaves

Marinate fish in tamarind for ½ an hour. Heat oil, add onion, curry leaves, spices then ginger, garlic, curry powder, turmeric and salt and cook until onion is browned then add tomato paste. Drop in fish gently and turn once. Add coriander when fish is cooked. Serve with rice and tamarind chutney.

Fried Fish

Mum had a reputation with family and friends for perfecting the flavours in the spice combination to make her sublime fried fish. Speaking fondly, the fish dish will invariably be brought into conversations at gatherings.

SERVES 4

- 500g snapper or flathead fillets
- 4 tablespoons tamarind pulp or juice of 1 lemon
- 2 teaspoons crushed ginger
- 4 cloves crushed garlic
- ¼ teaspoon chilli powder
- 2 dessertspoons curry powder
- 1 heaped teaspoon turmeric
- 1 teaspoon salt
- ½ cup flour
- Oil for deep frying

Marinate fish in tamarind for ½ an hour. Add water to spices to make a paste and add fish to the mixture. Coat fish in spice mixture, cover with flour and deep fry. Serve with tamarind chutney as a snack or with dhal and rice as a meal.

VEGETABLES

Potato Curry

SERVES 4–6

- 3 medium-sized potatoes
- 1 small chopped onion
- 8 tablespoons oil
- 3 cloves crushed garlic
- 2 teaspoons turmeric
- 1 teaspoon cumin powder
- ½ teaspoon asafoetida
- 1 teaspoon mustard seeds
- ½ teaspoon fenugreek seeds
- 1 teaspoon salt
- ½ teaspoon chilli powder
- 1 tablespoon chopped coriander leaves

Heat oil, fry onion with mustard and fenugreek seeds. Add other ingredients and cook until onion is lightly browned. Add potato and cook until tender.

VARIATIONS

This is a basic recipe for vegetable curries. Omit turmeric when using spinach, choraiya (green vegetable available in Fiji), eggplant, zucchini or rhubarb and tomato.

Pumpkin Curry

SERVES 4

- 4 tablespoons oil
- ½ chopped butternut pumpkin
- 1 small chopped onion
- 3 cloves crushed garlic
- ½ teaspoon crushed ginger
- ¼ teaspoon asafoetida
- 2 teaspoons turmeric
- ½ teaspoon fenugreek seeds
- ½ teaspoon cumin seeds
- ¼ teaspoon ajwain
- ½ teaspoon salt
- ½ teaspoon chilli powder or 1 whole chilli
- Juice of 1 small lemon or equivalent tamarind pulp with ½ teaspoon sugar
- ½ teaspoon mustard seeds
- 6–10 curry leaves

Fry onion and curry leaves in oil with fenugreek, mustard, cumin seeds and ajwain. Add asafoetida, ginger, garlic, salt, turmeric and chilli. Include diced pumpkin. When pumpkin is almost cooked (mushy), add lemon juice.

Chickpea Curry

SERVES 4–6

- 4 tablespoons oil
- 3 small potatoes, boiled and cubed
- 2 cups chickpeas (tinned with liquid removed or soak dried chickpeas overnight and boil for 45 minutes)
- 1 small finely chopped onion
- 3 cloves crushed garlic
- ½ teaspoon crushed ginger
- ½ teaspoon asafoetida
- ½ teaspoon fenugreek seeds
- ½ teaspoon mustard seeds
- ½ teaspoon cumin seeds
- 2 teaspoons turmeric
- 1 ½ teaspoons curry powder
- 6–8 curry leaves
- 1 ½ teaspoons salt
- 1 whole chilli or ½ teaspoon chilli powder
- Juice of 1 small lemon or 3 chopped tomatoes
- 2 tablespoon chopped coriander leaves

Fry onions in oil until browned. Add curry leaves, fenugreek, mustard and cumin seeds. Then add ginger, garlic, chilli, turmeric, curry powder and asafoetida. If tomato is preferred, add at this stage. Mix in chickpeas and cook until almost tender then add potatoes. Add salt and mix in lemon juice and chopped coriander leaves.

VARIATION

Substitute chickpea for brown lentils, green peas or black-eye beans. Dried ingredients will need to be soaked for a few hours and boiled first.

Tomato and Bean Chutney

SERVES 4–6

- 400g tinned tomatoes
- 1 small sliced onion
- 4 tablespoons oil
- ½ teaspoon crushed garlic
- ½ teaspoon crushed ginger
- 1 teaspoon mustard seeds
- ½ teaspoon cumin seeds
- ½ teaspoon fenugreek seeds
- 1 teaspoon salt
- 1 whole chilli
- 8 curry leaves
- 1 tablespoon chopped coriander leaves
- ½ cup sliced frozen beans

Heat oil, fry onion with mustard, cumin, fenugreek seeds and curry leaves. Add garlic, ginger, salt and chilli, cooking until onion is lightly browned, then add tomatoes and cook until mixture starts to thicken, add beans. Garnish with coriander leaves. Without the beans, serve as tomato chutney.

Dhal

Lentil soup is highly nutritious and economical, a staple food.

SERVES 6–8

3 tablespoons ghee or olive oil
1 cup split chickpea (channa dhal)
1 cup split pigeon pea (tur dhal)
6 cups water
1 small finely chopped onion
Vegetables: 3 sliced tomatoes,
  1 sliced carrot or 1 cup diced
  pumpkin or spinach
3 cloves crushed garlic
½ teaspoon crushed ginger
½ teaspoon asafoetida
¼ teaspoon fenugreek seeds
½ teaspoon mustard seeds
½ teaspoon cumin seeds
6–10 curry leaves
2 teaspoons turmeric
1 teaspoon sambhaar powder (for a
  spicy dhal)
2 tablespoons chopped coriander
  leaves
1 ½ teaspoons salt
½ teaspoon chilli powder
Juice of 1 small lemon

Soak lentils in water for an hour, discard water. Boil lentils in water with turmeric, chilli, vegetables, sambhaar powder and salt. When lentils are soft, add lemon juice. Heat oil, add onions, cumin, fenugreek, mustard seeds and curry leaves. Add ginger, garlic, asafoetida and then lentil mixture. Lastly, add coriander leaves and stir. Dhal is a common dish at lunch time, served with 1–2 vegetables and pickle or raita and rice.

VARIATIONS
  A variety of lentils can be used such as red lentil, split peas and mung beans.

Kadhi

A preparation of spicy curd mixture thickened with chickpea flour which can be enhanced with a simplified version of pakoras. I have selected a Gujerati version for the sweet-sour flavour which is so typical of the cooking style. An appetising vegetarian meal and a most pleasurable way of eating yoghurt.

SERVES 4

- 1 cup yoghurt
- ¼ teaspoon turmeric
- Pinch of asafoetida
- ½ teaspoon mustard seeds
- ½ teaspoon cumin seeds
- ½ chopped onion
- 6 curry leaves
- ½ teaspoon crushed garlic
- ½ teaspoon crushed ginger
- 1 tablespoon chickpea flour (besan)
- ½ teaspoon salt
- 2 cups water
- ½ chopped dried or green chilli
- 1 tablespoon oil or ghee
- 4 cloves
- 1 tablespoon chopped coriander leaves
- 1 tablespoon caster sugar

Combine yoghurt, turmeric, garlic, ginger, chickpea flour, salt and water. Heat oil, add cumin and mustard seeds, onion, chilli, cloves, curry leaves and asafoetida. When slightly browned, add yoghurt mixture and sugar. Lower heat, stirring constantly until mixture starts to boil. Leave uncovered for a few minutes and garnish with coriander leaves. Serve with rice, choice of vegetable dishes and a salad.

Sambhaar

Zesty South Indian dhal with vegetables.

SERVES 6

- 1 cup split pigeon pea (tur dhal)
- 3 cups water
- 1 teaspoon salt
- ¼ teaspoon turmeric
- 3 dessertspoons oil
- 1 cup vegetables (beans or carrot slices)
- 7 curry leaves
- 3 cloves crushed garlic
- 2 dessertspoons tamarind pulp
- 2 dessertspoons sambhaar powder
- 1 dessertspoon grated coconut
- ½ teaspoon mustard seeds
- 2 red dry chillies
- ¼ teaspoon asafoetida
- Coriander leaves for garnish

Cook lentil in water with turmeric and 1 dessertspoon oil until soft and mushy. Add vegetables, tamarind and salt. Add sambhaar powder and cook for 10–15 minutes, then add coconut. Heat the rest of the oil and add mustard seeds, chilli, asafoetida, garlic and curry leaves and pour into sambhaar mix. Garnish and serve with rice, dosa or idli.

Rasam

Tangy and flavoursome South Indian soup.

SERVES 4–6

- 2 cups water
- 1 small sliced onion
- 1 medium chopped tomato
- 2 tablespoons red lentil (masoor dhal, include if a thick consistency is required)
- 2 tablespoons oil or ghee
- 1 teaspoon turmeric
- 1 teaspoon cumin seeds
- 1 teaspoon mustard seeds
- ½ teaspoon black pepper
- 3–4 cloves crushed garlic
- ¼ teaspoon asafoetida
- 1 tablespoon tamarind pulp
- ½ teaspoon salt
- ¼ teaspoon chilli powder
- 6 curry leaves

To the tamarind mixed in water, add salt, cumin, pepper and garlic. Fry curry leaves in oil and add mustard seeds, onion and lentil. Then add turmeric, asafoetida, chilli and tomato and cook for a few minutes. Add tamarind mixture and stir. Cook for 10 minutes and serve with rice and a chutney.

Palusami

Baked parcels of taro leaves containing coconut cream, onion and meat filling – a favourite dish in several Pacific Islands. The taste is unique, particularly if cooked in a traditional Pacific Island earth oven.

SERVES 4–6

- 6–8 young taro leaves
- 1 chopped onion
- 2–3 tomatoes
- 500g fish or corned meat
- 1–2 chopped chillies
- Coconut milk from 3 coconuts or 2–3 cups coconut cream
- Juice of 1 lemon

Take 4–6 washed fresh taro leaves placing the largest on the outside. Into the centre put 1–2 teaspoons chopped onion, sliced tomato and chilli and about one cup of coconut cream, lemon juice plus a couple of tablespoons of fish and a sprinkle of salt. Fold the leaves carefully.

Wrap each taro leaf bundle in a piece of banana leaf softened by scalding in boiling water. Wrap the parcels in aluminium foil, moisten the outside of the leaves so they don't stick to the foil during cooking. Bake at 180–200 °C for 1 hour. This is a meal on its own with salad or if cooked without fish or meat, it can be served with a baked meat dish.

ACCOMPANIMENTS

Avocado Chutney/Dip

SERVES 4–6

- 1 medium avocado
- 1 small grated or chopped onion
- 1 clove crushed garlic
- 1 teaspoon cumin powder
- Juice of ½ lemon
- 1 dessertspoon chopped basil
- 1 dessertspoon chopped coriander
- 1 dessertspoon chopped mint
- 1 dessertspoon chopped dill
- 1 teaspoon salt
- ½ teaspoon chilli powder

Mash avocado with lemon juice, add all ingredients except the herbs. Blend, then add the four herbs. If you prefer chunky pieces, omit blending and simply mash. Serve as a dip with crackers or sliced vegetables such as carrots or as a chutney with curries. Include all four herbs or a few.

Coriander or Mint Chutney

SERVES 6–8

- 1 cup chopped coriander or mint
- 1 clove crushed garlic
- 1 diced tomato
- ½ teaspoon cumin powder
- ½ teaspoon salt
- ¼ teaspoon chilli powder

Blend all ingredients on high. A refreshing complement to most curries.

VARIATION

Boiled rhubarb may be added to the mint chutney.

Tomato and Cucumber Salad

SERVES 4–6

- 1 cup diced tomatoes
- 1 cup diced cucumber
- ¼ chopped onion
- Dash of vinegar (optional)
- ½ teaspoon salt
- 1 chilli, seeded and chopped
- 2 tablespoons chopped coriander

Mix all ingredients. Add a dash of vinegar if desired. Complements meat or vegetarian dishes nicely.

Raita

Refreshing yoghurt and cucumber salad.

SERVES 8–10

- 1 ½ cups plain yoghurt
- 1 small cucumber
- ½ teaspoon salt
- ½ teaspoon cumin powder
- 1 clove crushed garlic
- Coriander leaves for garnish

Grate cucumber and stir into yoghurt together with other ingredients.

Chilli Relish

Lively relish shared by Wally.

FILLS 2 SMALL JARS

    1 ½ cups hot chillies

    1 ½ cups onions

    1 cup white vinegar

    1 tablespoon mustard seeds

    1 tablespoon curry powder

    ½ cup caster sugar

    1 tablespoon salt

    1 dessertspoon cornflour

Mince chillies and onions. Place mixture in saucepan with other ingredients and boil for 15 minutes. Thicken with cornflour mixed with a little vinegar. Boil then simmer for 3 minutes. Cool and bottle.

VARIATIONS

    Green tomatoes or chokos may be used in lieu of chillies.

Carrot Pickle

Popular with my children and friends ever since I introduced this, we can never run out of it! I believe the recipe was bequeathed from Rita Mami, my maternal aunt.

FILLS 4 SMALL JARS

- 4 large grated carrots
- 1 dessertspoon pickle masala
- 8 cloves crushed garlic
- 1 dessertspoon mustard seeds
- 1 cup oil
- 5 dessertspoons salt (adjust to taste)
- 6 minced hot chillies (adjust to taste)
- 6 dessertspoons lemon juice (adjust to taste)

PICKLE MASALA

- 3 tablespoons fennel seeds
- 1 teaspoon ajwain
- 1 tablespoon fenugreek seeds
- 1 teaspoon nigella seeds
- 4 tablespoon cumin seeds

Roast spices for pickle and grind to a powder. Heat oil, add mustard seeds, garlic, salt, chilli and then carrots. When carrot is half cooked, add lemon juice, and when almost cooked, add masala. Cook for approximately 45 minutes in total. Bottle and refrigerate.

Coconut Chutney

An ideal accompaniment to South Indian meals; however, goes splendidly with many meat and vegetable dishes.

SERVES 8–10

- ½ grated coconut or 1 cup desiccated coconut
- ½ teaspoon cumin seeds
- 1 clove crushed garlic
- ¼ teaspoon chilli powder
- 1 teaspoon sesame seeds
- 1 tablespoon chopped mint or coriander leaves
- ¼ teaspoon salt
- 2-3 dessertspoons plain yoghurt (optional)

Dry roast grated coconut, cumin and sesame seeds. Add garlic, chilli and salt. Add mint and blend. Mix in yoghurt.

Tamarind Chutney

Zingy dipping sauce or chutney, you can never have enough of this!

FILLS 3 JARS

- 1 cup tamarind pulp
- 2 cups water
- ¼ cup caster sugar (adjust to taste)
- 1 ½ –2 teaspoons salt (adjust to taste)
- 6 minced hot chillies
- 3 tablespoons oil
- 3–5 curry leaves
- 2 teaspoons crushed ginger
- 4 cloves crushed garlic
- 1 teaspoon combined cumin, fenugreek and mustard seeds (roasted and ground)

To prepare pulp, soak tamarind in water for approximately 1 hour, then squeeze as much pulp as possible discarding skin. Heat oil and fry ginger, garlic, combined spice mixture and chillies until fried and separated from oil. Add curry leaves, fry for a few seconds then add the tamarind pulp and salt. Cook until the mixture starts to thicken, add sugar and stir well cooking until it reaches almost desired consistency for chutney. Stir in the ground spices. Cool and bottle.

RICE / BREADS

Plain Rice

SERVES 8
  1 cup washed rice
  6 cups water

Place rice and water in pot on high heat to boil. Slow down heat when it comes to boil, stir occasionally. When rice is ¾ or almost cooked, drain in a colander. Switch off the stove. When rice is well drained, return to the pot. Place pot on stove and leave to steam, stir twice.

RICE VARIATIONS
  Cooked rice can be enhanced as follows, vary the ingredients according to your preference.

  Curd Rice: Fry in 2 tablespoons oil, ½ teaspoon crushed ginger, 6 curry leaves, 1 green chilli, ½ teaspoon mustard seeds and 1 tablespoon split chickpea (channa dhal). Add to 2 cups boiled rice with 1 tablespoon of chopped coriander leaves, 1 cup yoghurt and ¼ teaspoon salt. With steamed vegetables such as beans, this is a nutritious meal in its own right.

  Tamarind Rice: Add 4 cardamom pods, 1 cinnamon stick, 1 teaspoon curry powder, 2 dry red chillies, ½ teaspoon salt, ½ teaspoon crushed garlic, ½ teaspoon crushed ginger, 6 curry leaves, ¼ cup cashew nuts, 1 teaspoon sesame seeds, ½ cup cooked chickpeas to 2 tablespoons hot ghee. Add 2 cups boiled rice and 2 tablespoons tamarind pulp. Served with a salad, this is a most appealing meal.

  Tomato Rice: To hot ghee, add ½ teaspoon cumin seeds, ½ teaspoon crushed garlic, ½ teaspoon crushed ginger, ½ teaspoon salt, ½ teaspoon chilli powder and ½ cup pureed onion. Add 2 tablespoons tomato paste and 2 cups boiled rice. Adding colour and classic flavour to a meal, the dish beautifully complements barbeques as well.

Lemon Rice: Fry in ghee, ½ teaspoon mustard seeds, rind of 1 large lemon, 1 teaspoon turmeric, ½ teaspoon salt, 2 dry red chillies and ½ teaspoon crushed garlic. Add 2 tablespoons lemon juice and 2 cups boiled rice. A stylish flavour combination to enthral your dinner guests!

Khicheri

Creamy rice and lentil meal served with yoghurt – easy to prepare and nutritious. Young children can be introduced to this meal without all the spices except turmeric. The ultimate comfort food as congee is for the Chinese.

SERVES 4

- 1 cup rice (works best with glutinous rice)
- ¼ cup red lentil (masoor dhal)
- 1 medium chopped potato
- ½ chopped carrot
- 1 teaspoon salt
- 2 dessertspoons ghee
- 1 teaspoon turmeric
- ½ chopped onion
- 2 cloves chopped garlic
- 1 teaspoon ground cardamom (optional)
- ½ teaspoon cumin seeds
- 3 cloves or 1½ teaspoon garam masala
- Chilli to taste

Soak rice and red lentil for ½ hour. Heat ghee, add cumin seeds and cloves. Add onion, garlic, turmeric and cardamom. Drain pre-soaked rice and red lentil and add to hot ghee with vegetables and add salt. Fry for a few minutes, add 2 cups water and more if required. Simmer until cooked to a creamy consistency.

VARIATIONS

Other vegetables that can be added are spinach and cauliflower.

Roti or Chapati

A flatbread cooked on a griddle.

SERVES 6

- 1 cup plain flour
- 1 dessertspoon ghee or oil, additional for applying when cooked
- ½ – ¾ cup hot water
- ½ cup wholemeal flour

Mix both flour and rub in ghee or oil. Adding hot water make a pliable dough. Knead well for 5 minutes and leave for ½ an hour. Divide into 6 pieces, make into balls, flatten and roll in a little flour. Taking each one, pat lightly between fingers and roll into a circle 14 cm in diameter. Cook on a hot griddle. Leave on one side for a few seconds, turn and cook on the other side. Whilst pressing lightly with the help of a paper towel, the roti should rise. Rub a little ghee or oil on each side. Serve with a variety of curries.

Puri

Deep-fried bread, a must for festive occasions!

SERVES 10

- 1 cup wholemeal flour
- 1 cup plain flour
- ½ teaspoon salt
- 1 tablespoon ghee, additional for deep frying
- ¾ cup cold water

Mix salt and both flour and rub in ghee. Adding cold water, make a pliable dough and knead well. Rub a drop of ghee around the dough to prevent it from sticking. Leave covered for ½ to 2 hours. Divide into approximately 10 portions, making into balls. Roll into a circle 12 cm in diameter. Deep fry both sides in ghee until lightly browned. Puris are best served hot with curries.

Savoury Puri

SERVES 8

- 2 cups plain flour
- 1 cup water
- 1 dessertspoon sesame seeds
- 1 clove crushed garlic
- ½ teaspoon chilli powder
- 1 teaspoon turmeric
- ½ teaspoon ajwain
- 1 teaspoon salt
- 1 dessertspoon oil, additional for deep frying

Mix turmeric and salt in water. Mix all dry ingredients and add 1 dessertspoon oil. Make a stiff dough with water mixture. Cut, roll into circles of 12 cm diameter and deep fry. Serve with curries or make small ones to have as a snack.

Bhatura

Fermented puris, so rich and delectable! Introduced to us by Aunty Ratna.

SERVES 8

- Approximately 2 cups self-raising flour
- 1 cup plain yoghurt
- ½ teaspoon salt
- ½ teaspoon sesame seeds
- ½ teaspoon crushed cumin seeds
- ½ teaspoon poppy seeds
- Oil for deep frying

Mix all ingredients and leave for 2–3 hours. Make into small balls, roll into circles of 12 cm diameter and deep fry. Bhatura beautifully enhances a dish of chicken or chickpea curry.

Idli

Steamed, savoury rice cakes to be taken with richly spiced dishes. This recipe is for rava idli as it is made with semolina – simple and tasty.

SERVES 4

- 1 cup coarse semolina
- 1 cup plain yoghurt
- ½ grated carrot
- ½ grated zucchini
- 1 dessertspoon chopped coriander leaves
- 2 small chopped chillies
- ½ teaspoon mustard seeds
- 2 teaspoons baking powder
- 1 teaspoon salt
- 2 dessertspoons oil
- 1 clove crushed garlic

Fry garlic, chillies and mustard seeds in oil. Add to the rest of the ingredients. Leave for an hour and steam in an oil-greased idli pot for 10–12 minutes. Serve with sambhaar and coconut chutney for a meal or simply as a snack filled with coconut chutney.

Dosa

Savoury, rice crepe - mouth-watering and crispy. A simple and quick version.

SERVES 4

- 1 cup fine semolina or ½ cup flour (or rice flour) and ½ cup semolina
- ½ cup plain yoghurt
- 1 tablespoon grated carrot or 1 tablespoon grated zucchini
- Chopped coriander leaves (optional)
- 1 clove crushed garlic
- 2 small chopped chillies
- ½ teaspoon baking powder
- Water
- ¼ teaspoon salt
- Oil for frying

Mix all ingredients and leave for a few hours. Cook as for pancakes over a hot oiled plate. Serve with potato curry to enjoy masala dosa. Other accompaniments are coconut chutney and sambhaar.

DESSERT/SWEETS

Easy Fruit Cake

Simply had to include this family favourite from my Fua (paternal aunt).

SERVES 10–12

- 1 cup brown sugar
- 450g mixed fruit
- 1 teaspoon baking soda
- 225g butter
- 1 teaspoon grated nutmeg
- 2 eggs
- 2 cups self-raising flour
- ½ cup slivered almonds
- 1 dessertspoon vanilla essence
- 1 dessertspoon brandy

Add 1 cup boiling water to sugar, mixed fruit, baking soda and butter. Add other ingredients and pour mixture into lined cake tin. Bake at 180°C for 40–45 minutes. The cake will keep fresh for days at room temperature and can be enjoyed at Christmas or any other occasion.

One Egg Sponge Cake

Another family favourite from Fua featuring a voluptuous cake, although not your quintessential light and fluffy sponge.

SERVES 8–10

- 60g butter
- ¾ cup warm milk
- ¾ cup caster sugar
- 1 egg
- 1 teaspoon vanilla essence
- 1 cup plain flour
- 1 teaspoon baking powder

Cream butter, sugar and egg at high speed using an electric beater. Stir in dry ingredients and milk. Place in lined tin and bake at 200°C for 30 minutes. When cooled, spread with whipped cream and garnish with strawberries before serving.

Banana Cake

A much-cherished recipe from Aunty Margaret.

SERVES 8–10

    2 ripe bananas
    1 egg
    1 heaped cup flour
    1 teaspoon baking powder
    1 teaspoon baking soda
    115g butter
    1 cup caster sugar
    3 tablespoons milk

Mash bananas, add milk and baking soda. Cream butter and sugar, fold in beaten egg, banana mixture, flour and baking powder. Pour into lined baking tin and bake at 180°C for 45 minutes. Serve with tea.

Scones

A specialty from Kara.

MAKES APPROXIMATELY 10–15

- 2 cups flour
- 1 heaped teaspoon custard powder
- 1 heaped teaspoon milk powder
- 2 teaspoons baking powder
- 2 tablespoons caster sugar
- 50g butter
- 1 egg
- ¼ cup water

Preheat oven to 200°C. Rub butter into sifted flour, baking powder, custard and milk powders then mix in sugar. Fold in egg and water to make a soft dough and knead on a lightly floured surface until smooth. Pat until 2 cm thick and cut out rounds. Place on prepared baking tray. Bake for 12–15 minutes. Serve with jam and cream.

Corny Biscuits

Children's party treat compliments of Aunty Margaret!

MAKES APPROXIMATELY 10–15

- 120g cornflakes
- 1 egg
- 2 cups flour
- 1 teaspoon baking powder
- 4 tablespoons caster sugar
- 175g butter
- 2 tablespoons sultanas (optional)

Mix butter and sugar. Fold in egg, flour and baking powder. Lastly, add sultanas and cornflakes, making the mixture into roughly shaped balls, and bake at 200°C for 30 minutes.

American Crunch

A much-loved slice passed on from Dorothy and Susan Walker, friends in Fiji.

MAKES APPROXIMATELY 20

- 2 cups flour
- 2 teaspoons baking powder
- 8 tablespoons caster sugar
- 225g butter
- 1 cup desiccated coconut
- ½ teaspoon salt
- 4 teaspoons cocoa

Preheat oven to 180°C. Sift flour, cocoa, baking powder and salt. Add sugar and coconut. Melt butter and add to dry ingredients. Put mixture in a greased tin and press evenly. Place tray on second shelf and bake for 50 minutes with oven switched off.

ICING

- 225 icing sugar
- ½ cup water
- 25g melted butter
- 2 tablespoons cocoa

Mix icing sugar and cocoa into butter and water. Spread on slice when cooled.

Gulgula

Mini donuts, easily prepared iconic sweet.

MAKES APPROXIMATELY 20

1 cup self-raising flour	1 beaten egg
½ cup caster sugar	½ cup milk or as required
½ teaspoon finely ground cardamom	¼ cup sultanas
1 teaspoon vanilla essence	Ghee or oil for deep frying

Mix all ingredients and deep fry in ghee or oil in dessertspoonful until golden brown. Serve warm.

VARIATIONS

Alternatively, instead of vanilla and sultanas, add ½ cup mashed banana or ½ cup boiled and mashed pumpkin.

Gulab Jamun

Deep-fried spongy milk balls, one of the most popular Indian sweets which can also be made with milk powder.

MAKES APPROXIMATELY 40–50

- 1 tin condensed milk
- 2 cups plain flour
- 2 tablespoons baking powder
- ½ teaspoon grated nutmeg
- 2 teaspoons ground cardamom
- 4 tablespoons ghee, additional for deep frying

SYRUP

- 4 cups water
- 4 cups caster sugar

Dissolve sugar in water and boil for 5 minutes to make syrup. Syrup is ready when it drops like thread. Leave aside.

Pour condensed milk in bowl, add ghee, nutmeg and cardamom and mix well. Add sifted flour and baking powder and make into a dough, add more flour if required. Make into balls or little sausage shapes. Deep fry in ghee and place in syrup. Take the batch out from syrup when the next batch is ready to go in. Serve with syrup or Greek-style yoghurt or on their own.

Barfi

Milk and coconut slice which can also be made with condensed milk or cottage cheese. I have included an easy-to-prepare, melt-in-the-mouth recipe.

MAKES APPROXIMATELY 40–50

- 1 cup caster sugar
- ½ cup grated coconut
- 1 cup milk powder
- ½ teaspoon ground cardamom
- 2 tablespoons ghee
- 1 teaspoon vanilla essence
- ½ cup chopped almonds for garnish

Cook sugar, ghee and coconut with vanilla until mixture is ready to set. Remove from cooktop and add milk and cardamom. Place mixture into a greased tray and cut into squares when partially set and garnish with almonds. Refrigerate to set fully and serve at room temperature. A much-loved Diwali treat!

Suji Ladoo

Buttery semolina balls. A favourite variation is made using chickpea flour with a different preparation method. I include the suji recipe as this was more commonly prepared at my home as a Diwali sweet.

MAKES APPROXIMATELY 20–30

- 1 cup fine semolina
- 1/3 cup plain flour
- ¾ cup icing sugar
- 1 teaspoon ground cardamom
- 1 tablespoon ghee, additional for binding and frying
- Milk for mixing

Rub ghee in semolina and flour, mix into a stiff dough with a little milk. Make into small puri shapes and fry in ghee until crisp. Pound or place puris in a food processor until mixture resembles semolina. Mix sugar with semolina mixture and add cardamom. Roll into small balls, binding with ghee. An awesome festive treat!

Sewai

Vermicelli pudding, creamy and luscious.

SERVES 8–10

- 2 cups broken sewai vermicelli
- 4 cups milk (amount can be altered depending on thickness required, vermicelli soaks up a lot of liquid)
- 2 tablespoons ghee
- 2 tablespoons caster sugar
- 6 whole or equivalent ground cardamom
- ½ teaspoon grated nutmeg
- ¼ cup slivered almonds
- ¼ cup sultanas or currants (optional)

Heat ghee, fry cardamom, add sultanas and cook until they puff up. Turn heat down, add vermicelli and toss around quickly for a minute to brown evenly. Omit this step if vermicelli has been roasted. Add milk, almonds, nutmeg and sugar and bring to boil slowly to ensure vermicelli is cooked. Sugar tends to burn if added prior to liquid. Serve warm.

VARIATIONS

Cinnamon or cloves can be substituted for cardamom and nutmeg.

Kheer

Rice pudding with subtle spices. In North India, kheer is a ritualistic offering just as payasam is in the South.

SERVES 6–8

- ½ –¾ cup glutinous rice
- ½ cup caster sugar
- 1 level teaspoon ground cardamom
- ½ teaspoon grated nutmeg
- ½ cup slivered almonds
- ¼ cup sultanas (optional)
- 6–8 cups milk
- 2 tablespoons butter or ghee

Heat butter in a pan and lightly roast the washed rice. Add milk and sultanas and gently bring to boil. Cook on gentle heat stirring often as milk tends to burn or boil over. This may take about an hour or more. Add sugar and almond and keep stirring often until the consistency is thick yet able to be poured. Mixture will get thicker on cooling. Add cardamom and nutmeg and stir well. Serve warm with evaporated milk if desired.

Halwa

Semolina confection, one of my favourite sweets.

SERVES 6–8

- 1 cup coarse semolina
- 3 cups milk
- 1 cup caster sugar
- ¼ cup slivered almonds
- ½ teaspoon ground cardamom
- 3 dessertspoons sultanas or other dried fruit
- 2–3 tablespoons ghee

Fry semolina in ghee. Add milk, cardamom, almonds, sugar and sultanas stirring until semolina is cooked. Halwa can be served with fruit such as passionfruit if desired or on its own.

Semolina Pudding

SERVES 6

½ cup fine semolina
2 ½ cups milk
½ cup caster sugar
2 eggs

1 tablespoon vanilla essence
½ teaspoon nutmeg
Butter

Roast sugar and semolina. Mix egg beaten with milk and vanilla to semolina mixture. Top with butter chunks and nutmeg and bake until browned. Serve with fruit or evaporated milk.

Lakri Mithai

Sugar-coated confection popular with all ages.

MAKES APPROXIMATELY 50–60 PIECES

- 2 cups plain flour
- 2 heaped dessertspoons sesame seeds
- ½ dessertspoon poppy seeds
- ½ – ¾ cup water
- Oil for deep frying

SYRUP

- 1 ½ cups raw sugar
- ¾ cup water

To make syrup, cook sugar and water until the mixture bubbles, leave aside. Mix dry ingredients with water. Break into 6 portions and roll out until ½ cm thick and then cut thinly. Deep fry in oil and drop in syrup. This is a favourite sweet prepared during Diwali.

Kulfi

Fragrant ice cream, sumptuous and easy-to-prepare dessert which can be made in advance and enjoyed on many occasions.

SERVES 12–15

- 1 tin condensed milk
- 1–2 tins evaporated milk
- 2–3 slices white bread with crust removed (optional)
- Fruit (pulp of 1 mango)
- Ground cardamom for garnish
- Pistachio or slivered almond for garnish
- Few drops vanilla essence or rosewater (optional)

Blend condensed and evaporated milk with bread, fruit, vanilla and cardamom. Garnish with pistachio and cardamom. Freeze and serve with fresh fruit.

Payasam

Festive milk pudding, expect to have payasam if attending a South Indian wedding. The combination of dhal, milks and spices produces a formidable dessert! As well as being integral to any festive meal, payasam is an important ritualistic offering.

SERVES 8–10

- ½ cup yellow mung dhal
- 1 cup coconut milk
- ½ cup evaporated milk
- ½ teaspoon dried ginger powder (sonth)
- ½ teaspoon grated nutmeg
- ¼ cup sago
- 3 dessertspoons caster sugar
- ¼ cup slivered almonds
- 2 tablespoons ghee
- 5 crushed cardamom

Fry yellow mung dhal in ghee, then boil in evaporated and coconut milk until it melts. Add the sago and when it is almost cooked, add all other ingredients. Serve warm.

Semolina Payasam

A most promising variation on payasam.

SERVES 6–8

½ cup coarse semolina
2 dessertspoons ghee
1½ cups milk
2 dessertspoons slivered almonds
1/3 cup caster sugar
½ teaspoon ground nutmeg
½ teaspoon ground cardamom
¼ teaspoon dried ginger powder (sonth)

Fry semolina in ghee. Add other ingredients and simmer until semolina is cooked. Serve warm or at room temperature.

Vakalolo

Fijian tapioca and coconut cake

MAKES APPROXIMATELY 30 PIECES

- 1 ½ cups grated tapioca
- 1 ½ cups grated (or desiccated) coconut
- ½ cup brown sugar
- 1 cup powdered milk
- ½ teaspoon ground cardamom
- ½ teaspoon ground cinnamon

Mix all ingredients and steam for 1 hour in a steamer then bake at 180°C for 5 minutes. Slice and serve warm.

Purini

A Fijian cake to which our family in Fiji often treated us. Thanks to Vika and Tokasa for this delightful recipe.

MAKES APPROXIMATELY 20 PIECES

- 2 cups flour
- 1 ½ cups brown sugar
- 1 teaspoon baking soda
- 2 teaspoons baking powder
- 1 teaspoon vanilla essence
- 120g butter
- Coconut milk from 1 coconut or 1 cup coconut cream

Cook 1 ¼ cups sugar until it gets golden brown, add ½ cup hot water. When mixture boils, add coconut milk and boil for 5 minutes. Add half the butter and cool. Sift flour, baking powder, baking soda and rub in remaining butter. Add ¼ cup sugar. When syrup is cooled, add vanilla and mix in flour mixture gradually. Pour into a greased pudding tin and steam in a steaming pot for approximately 1 hour, 15 minutes. Add additional hot water to pot if required. Insert a skewer in the pudding to check if it is cooked; if there is no residue then pudding is ready.

MASALA

Curry Powder

2 cups coriander seeds
3 tablespoons cumin seeds
2 tablespoons fenugreek seeds

2 tablespoons fennel seeds
1 ½ tablespoons rice

Roast all ingredients and grind together.

Garam Masala

2 tablespoons fennel seeds
1 dozen cloves
1 dozen cardamom

2 cinnamon sticks
6–8 star anise

Roast all ingredients and grind together.

Tea Masala

1 teaspoon ginger powder
1 teaspoon white pepper
½ teaspoon ground cardamom

½ teaspoon grated nutmeg
½ teaspoon ground clove or cinnamon

Mix all ingredients and grind.

BEVERAGES

Masala Chai

Spicy and milky tea.

1 teaspoon black tea	¼ teaspoon tea masala
Milk to taste	(see Tea Masala)
Sugar to taste	

Add masala and tea to teapot with 1 cup boiling water. Serve with milk and sugar.

Pineapple and Mint Juice

Do not discard pineapple skins after preparing a fruit salad. Boil with mint leaves for a most refreshing and inviting beverage. This is one of Aunty Ratna's beautiful recommendations.

SERVES 6–8

- Skin of 1 pineapple
- 6 sprigs mint
- Sugar to taste

There is more goodness left to enjoy from the pineapple by boiling the skin and mint leaves for an hour. Add sugar, discard pineapple skin and mint leaves, serving the juice chilled.

Nimbu Pani or Sharbat

Refreshing lemon or lime thirst quencher

SERVES 4–6

    Juice of 2 lemons or limes
    4 tablespoons caster sugar
    ¼ teaspoon salt
    1 teaspoon ground pepper
    4 cups water

Mix all ingredients until sugar dissolves. Serve chilled with ice cubes and lemon or lime slices.

REMEDIES

Cough Mixture

2 cups milk
½ teaspoon ajwain
½ teaspoon black pepper

2 teaspoons ground ginger
1 teaspoon turmeric
Honey or sugar to taste

Boil all ingredients, sieve and drink a few times a day.

Cough Syrup

½ onion (cut in cross section)

Honey or raw sugar

Pour honey in onion centre. Take syrup 4–5 times a day as it flows from onion.

MENU PLANNER

Planning a menu for a dinner party requires some consideration – number of guests, dietary restrictions, balance of flavours, colours, textures and vegetarian and non-vegetarian dishes.

I have included a few suggestions for dinners, range of snacks for a cocktail party as well as a festive meal prepared on Diwali.

Dinner party Menu 1

Entrée:
Fried Fish with Tamarind Chutney

Main:
Lamb Curry
Dhal
Eggplant Curry (to Potato Curry recipe, add 2 chopped eggplants,
halving the quantity of potatoes)
Tomato and Bean Chutney
Raita
Plain Rice and Rotis

Dessert:
Semolina Payasam

♦♦♦

Dinner party Menu 2

Entrée:
Bhajia with Chilli Relish

Main:
Chicken Curry
Chickpea Curry
Cauliflower curry (using Potato Curry recipe,
substitute potatoes with 3 cups cauliflower florets)
Coconut Chutney
Tomato and Cucumber Salad
Lemon Rice and Puris

Dessert:
Kulfi with seasonal fruit

♦ ♦ ♦

Diwali Menu

A generous menu is the custom so include a few savouries, many vegetarian dishes and an assortment of sweets. The variety of savouries and sweets are conscientiously prepared and exchanged amongst family and friends.

Savouries:
Dhokla with Coconut Chutney
Vegetarian Samosas
Nimki

Mains:
Pea Curry (substitute pea for chickpea in Chickpea Curry recipe)

Pumpkin Curry

Potato and Snakebean Curry (to Potato Curry recipe,
add 1 bundle chopped snakebean, halving the quantity of potatoes)

Kadhi

Carrot Pickle

Mint Chutney

Tomato Rice and Bhatura

Sweets:
Barfi
Gulab Jamun
Halwa

♦ ♦ ♦

Cocktail Snacks

Mixed Bhuja (assortment of peas, peanuts and lentil-based savouries obtained from supermarkets or Indian groceries)

Avocado Chutney with Crackers

Pappadum served with Raita

Vegetarian or Meat Samosas with Chilli Relish

Saina

Eggplant, Potato and Prawns dipped in chickpea flour batter then deep-fried

Fried Fish with Tamarind Chutney

THE MASTER CHEF

Have you ever thought that you can cook
And thought you're pretty smart?
Well, here is one who kids himself,
Amusing all he has the art.

Bought books he did from shops galore,
Of cuisines from far and wide
And then to markets here and there
For recipes that's true and tried.

And then to Google and TV screen
For more of savoir-faire
So he could boast of main delights
And entrée of great personal flair.

Still to master, desserts and soups
And how to serve with class;
But, on the first of a one-man show,
His culinary tests were just a farce.

Undaunted he blamed the ignorant tastes
Of ignorant ones he dined,
Connoisseurs, be next his guests,
A feast he'll serve, each course defined.

He purchased this and flavoured that
All with a master's skill,
His style was eloquent, his touch supreme,

Not one morsel lacked a thrill.
And when his guests arrived to dine,
He beamed assured as a master chef
And as they sat to music charmed,
His bursting ego, to their praise, was deaf.

With deft aplomb he poured the wine,
Each course his style enhanced,
With cultured class his plates prevailed.
Their bewitching modes, his guests entranced.

And then the final crowning course,
Nectar braided with sumptuous pain;
With grand delight he served the last,
Never to be repeated again!

How great the applause the guests did give,
The chef stood tall and bowed,
The lights went out as he was bent
And a voice beside him showered.

Wakee, wakee, time to cook,
You've had a nice long rest,
I did my turn the night before;
Now, your turn to do your best!

Wally Kwan, 2009

My friend Wally who is 93, is admirable for the countless dinner parties he has catered for with a banquet to satisfy all palates. The richness of flavours, freshness of vegetables and array of colours are a feast to behold. The poem (yes, he can also add poetry to his many talents) from Wally is a testament to his warmth and lovingly prepared dishes.

GLOSSARY: HERBS AND SPICES

Many homes create their own spice mixture and various combinations catering for individual tastes and dishes. There will be different mixtures for meat and fish.

The major herbs and spices used in Indian cuisine are listed below together with some of their uses.

AJWAIN (carom) Equivalent name in English is not known. Ajwain has a bitter flavour, having digestive properties and belongs to the caraway family.

ASAFOETIDA (hing) Usually sold in powder form, having a distinctive pungent flavour and aroma mainly due to sulphur compounds. The herb has strong digestive properties.

CARDAMOM (illaichi) Known as 'The Queen of Spices' in India, there are two types of cardamoms – the stronger-flavoured green ones and the lesser-flavoured white cardamoms. The entire cardamom, including the husk, can be used in cooking. The spice has a complex flavour – sweet, floral and spicy. Cardamoms are an ingredient in garam masala and used in curries as well as sweets. The pods can be brewed with other spices in teas as a cold remedy and also chewed after meals as a digestive aid and breath sweetener.

CHILLI (mirch) Two types of chilli, green and red are used in curries. The colour and size are not a guide to the intensity of chillies. The fiery taste of green chillies is derived mainly from the white seeds. The skin in most cases has a pleasant flavour unlike the seeds. One way to reduce the heat of green chillies is to slit the chillies, remove the seeds, rubbing the inside with a little salt before washing the chillies. Those with an appreciation for extremely hot chillies will often eat them raw with meals.

Red chillies are sold whole or ground as chilli powder. Ground chilli has a more concentrated effect.

CINNAMON (dalchini) One of the oldest spices available, cinnamon is the aromatic bark of the cinnamon tree. Sometimes, the bark of the cassia tree is also sold as cinnamon as the taste is very similar. Ground cinnamon is an essential ingredient in garam masala. Cinnamon can be chewed as a breath sweetener and is also used in the making of sweets.

CLOVE (laung) Dried flower buds of the clove tree, cloves have strong, aromatic flavour and are included in garam masala. Clove oil has analgesic qualities and can be used as a remedy for toothaches. In masala chai, cloves are a predominant ingredient.

CORIANDER (dhania) One of the most versatile herbs, coriander is also known as cilantro. The fragrant leaves of the coriander are used as garnish, in salads or chutneys.

The seeds produce a fine aroma when roasted.

CUMIN (jira) Aromas emerge when the seeds are dry roasted or added to hot oil. The flavour is sharp and sour.

CURRY LEAVES (tejpatti or in Tamil, karuveppilai) The highly aromatic curry leaves release a fine aroma when fried in oil or simply added to a simmering meat dish.

FENNEL SEEDS (saunf) This fragrant spice tastes and smells like liquorice. The seeds are used to flavour pickles and can be chewed after meals as a digestive aid; they are also a breath freshener.

FENUGREEK (methi) The mustard-coloured seeds have an overpowering smell, are very bitter and used in small amounts.

The plant is a legume and the leaves are used as a vegetable or herb and not as strong as the seed.

GARLIC (lasun) A pungent flavouring agent, avoid over cooking garlic as it will acquire a bitter taste. It has therapeutic properties.

GINGER, FRESH (adrak) A rhizome, fresh ginger is often referred to as a 'root'. It is widely used in Indian cooking, having many uses such as preservative, therapeutic and flavouring.

GINGER, DRY (sonth) Powdered ginger with a strong aroma used in masala, tea and sweets like payasam.

MINT (pudina) Originally used as a medicinal herb, the leaves have a fresh, aromatic, sweet flavour with a cool aftertaste. It is favoured in chutneys especially with tomatoes and also used as a garnish.

MUSTARD SEED (sarso) Available in three colours – black, brown or white, the seeds release their flavours when fried in hot oil. The black seeds are the ones predominantly used. The seeds can also be used in pickles. Mustard seed oil is also used in cooking.

NUTMEG (jaiphal) A desirable spice in savouries and sweets such as kheer.

NIGELLA SEED (mangrel) A black, triangular-shaped seed used readily in pickles and it is also a herbal remedy.

PEPPERCORN, BLACK (kali mirch) Known as 'The King of Spices' in India, it is the fruit of the black pepper and can be used in spice mixtures. It aids in digestion and acts as a stimulant.

SAFFRON (kesar) The dried stamen of a crocus, saffron is the most expensive spice. It is highly aromatic, giving a yellowish-orange colour to dishes such as rice. It is also used in sweet preparation.

SESAME SEED (til) Both white and black seeds are used in savouries and sweets. Sesame oil is used in cooking.

TAMARIND (imli) The pulp of the tamarind pod is used after being soaked in warm water. It has a piquant and sour flavour and can be used for flavouring a spicy fish curry, rasam and makes a flavoursome pickle.

TURMERIC POWDER (haldi) Earthy, sharp flavour with digestive and antiseptic properties and used in many curry dishes. It is also used in Hindu religious ceremonies.

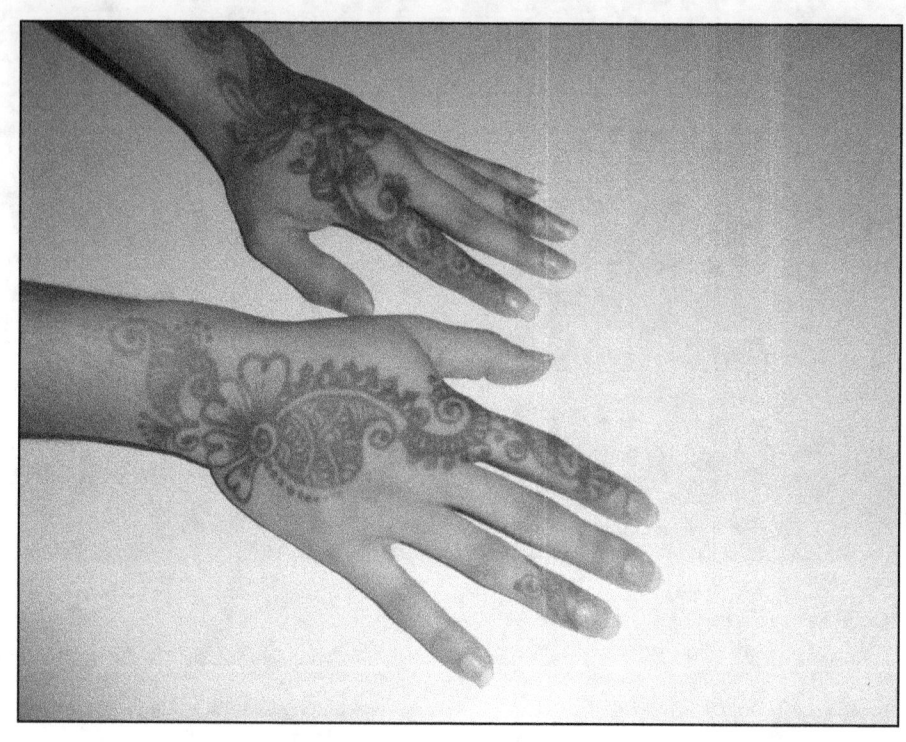

REFERENCES

Ali, A. 1981, 'Fiji: the Fiji Indian achievement', in Pacific Indians: profiles in 20 Pacific countries, ed R. Crocombe, Institute of Pacific Studies, University of the South Pacific in association with the Hanna Seidel Foundation, Suva, pp. 22-32.

Allende, I. 1998, Aphrodite: a memoir of the senses, Flamingo, [Australia].

Collingham, L. 2006, Curry: a tale of cooks and conquerors, Vintage Books, London.

David, E. 2010, At Elizabeth David's table: classic recipes and timeless kitchen wisdom, Harper Collins, New York.

Hemphill, I. 2002, Spice travels: a spice merchant's voyage of discovery, Pan Macmillan, Sydney.

Huntley, R. 2014, Does cooking matter? Penguin, Melbourne.

Johnson, K. 2017, 'Slow-cooking from the heart', The Sydney Morning Herald: Good weekend, 8 April, p. 25.

'Kitchen melodies – Curry', 1846, Punch, or The London Charivari, vol. 11, pp. 221, viewed 26 January 2018,
https://books.google.com.au/books?id=7n5EAAAAcAAJ&pg=PA221

Kurti, N. & Kurti, G. (eds.) 1997, But the crackling is superb: an anthology on food and drink by fellows and foreign members of The Royal Society, IOP Publishers, London.

Merchant, I. 1990, Ismael Merchant's Indian cuisine, Fireside, New York.
Monroe, J. 2005, Star of India: the spicy adventures of curry, Wiley, West Sussex, UK.

Morais, R. 2014, The hundred-foot journey, Allen & Unwin, Sydney.

Narayan, S. 2003, Monsoon diary: a memoir with recipes, Bantam Books, Sydney.

Nutta-Singh, J. T. 2008, Fiji Indian Chef: an insight into Indian culture plus 150 recipes, Zeus Publications, Burleigh M.D.C., Qld.

Pathak, M. 2007, Meena Pathak celebrates Indian cooking: 100 delicious recipes, 50 years of Patak's, New Holland, London.

Robbins, M. P. (ed.) 1987, The cook's quotation book: a literary feast, Robert Hale, London.

Seeto, L. 2014, 'Ancient Indian diet', The Fiji Times Online, 13 July, viewed 6 April 2017, < http://www.fijitimes.com/story.aspx?id=274228>.

Sen, C. 2009, Curry: a global history, Reaktion Books, London.

Subramani (ed.) 1979, The Indo-Fijian experience, University of Queensland Press, St Lucia, Qld.

'The joy of food' 2014, National Geographic, December, pp. 36-53.

Veerasawmy, E. P. 1969, Indian cookery, Grafton Books, London.

Wickramasinghe, P. & Selva Rajah, C. 2012, India: a journey for food lovers, Bay Books, [Sydney].

Wood, C. 2012, Love and hunger, Allen & Unwin, Sydney.

Woolf, V. 1929, A room of one's own, Hogarth Press, London.

ABOUT THE AUTHOR

Nalini Naidu, originally from Fiji, attended Waikato University in New Zealand and RMIT in Australia. She has established an extensive career in Knowledge Management and Information Technology whilst pursuing her enthusiasm for cooking, with a compelling interest in cultures and their associated food.

Her interest in cooking sparked during childhood as she assisted her mother in food preparation, memories that are relived as she prepares food with her two daughters. Since then she continued to cultivate her passion encompassing various aspects of food and cookery including nutrition, creativity, entertainment and the sheer joy whilst endeavouring to experiment with new concepts and explore food from a philosophical perspective.

Having participated in the art of various cooking styles and philosophies, Nalini is a true foodie, easily inspired by ingredients of the everyday and the less familiar, a journey that will no doubt continue for life.

'One cannot think well, love well, sleep well, if one has not dined well' (Woolf 1929, p. 28).

https://www.facebook.com/fijiindiancookbook/

ACKNOWLEDGEMENTS

To Mum, for she knew how to nourish, love and innovate. Thank you for the love of food, inspiration, succinct recollection of recipes and editorial support. Dad, appreciative of Mum's cooking, loved to share her passion by inviting one and all to celebrate her creations. My children, Anouschka and Nitasha, my rocks who have stood by me, testing my experiments or whims with unflagging enthusiasm. You all make me a better person, and hopefully cook, each day.

My heartiest appreciation to Wally Kwan for allowing me the privilege of including his poem, *The Master Chef* and sharing many of his recipes such as chilli relish and meals over the years, an unending inspiration.

Engaging in exquisite meals and acquiring recipes from family and various friends was a bonus for this book, although there may be a few recipes where the origin is uncertain or unknown. It is an honour to have had people in my life who had wonderful culinary skills. My sincerest gratitude to:

Maha Lakshmi, my paternal aunt, who was one of the greatest and most versatile cooks. She was respectfully sought after for huge wedding banquets where her competence was unsurpassed.

Ratna Krishnan, who to this day never ceases to amaze with her novel dishes and ideas, indeed a pleasure to dine at her home. Her food expertise across cultures is phenomenal.

Margaret Venkataya for her delightful cake and biscuit recipes which were very much and continue to be part of our lives. Graciously catering to all, she has quite a repertoire of skills from baking to a variety of Indian dishes.

Sudha Chandra displayed her talents whilst entertaining our family at her home and restaurant numerous times, always loving and caring. Remarkable in her creation of an array of dishes, she has won the affection of many.

The punchy carrot pickle complementing curries is attributed to Rita Raylu, the exquisite American crunch to Dorothy and Susan Walker, the light and fluffy scones to Kara and some very inviting Fijian dishes to Tokasa Duanalesu and her sister, Vika. My deep gratitude for the editorial assistance and constant encouragement from Anouschka Akerman, Chris Hagan, Bhagia Puran, Natalie Ritchie and Saroj Krishna – all willingly assisted, applying their aptitudes. Anouschka took time out of her busy schedule to devote to my needs. Chris Hagan generously provided guidance and support in innumerable ways. Bhagia's guidance with some recipes and culinary expertise was welcomed. Natalie provided immediate attention on publishing, with many suggestions. My family reminded me of some childhood dishes, with Padma Naidu reviewing my work and keeping the conversation alive. Martin Taylor provided invaluable insights into the publishing world, with admirable advice on book production.

I owe a great deal to my photographers. Kamlesh Chand spent countless hours editing and valiantly accommodated my various changes. My food has never looked better! Rikesh Krishna devoted much time with cover and kitchen gadget photographs, creating them with great finesse. Nitasha and Jan Akerman supported with photographic ideas and layout.

Thank you for the journey and belief in bringing me to this book.

I trust that I have given Fiji Indian food the recognition it deserves. In sharing a meal, we exchange conversations, forge relationships and discuss intimate matters in a trusting environment – we must continue the enduring tradition vital for our wellbeing.

www.ingramcontent.com/pod-product-compliance
Lightning Source LLC
Chambersburg PA
CBHW081358290426
44110CB00018B/2408